The Walt McDonald First-Book Series in Poetry
Rachel Mennies, *editor*

Foreword by Rachel Mennies

Lena

Cassie Pruyn

Texas Tech University Press

This book is typeset in Adobe Caslon Pro. The paper used in this book meets the minimum requirements of ANSI/NISO Z39.48-1992 (R1997). ∞

Designed by Kasey McBeath

Library of Congress Cataloging-in-Publication Data is on file with publisher.

17 18 19 20 21 22 23 24 25 / 9 8 7 6 5 4 3 2 1

Texas Tech University Press
Box 41037 | Lubbock, Texas 79409-1037 USA
800.832.4042 | ttup@ttu.edu | www.ttupress.org

Contents

III.

Series Editor's Foreword

Cassie Pruyn's *Lena*, winner of the 2017 Walt McDonald First-Book Prize in Poetry, furthers a centuries-old literary tradition: book as eponym for the beloved. Yet Lena, this collection's beloved, disappears from the speaker's life almost as soon as the book begins. A lush and unsparing first book, *Lena* asks readers to understand love—crucially, a first love, an erotic love—in the context not of a love lost but instead of an identity gained: we must consider not only "was she worth it?", but also "who has she made me?" The answer to this question unfurls masterfully across each of the book's three sections. In *Lena*, we traverse the latitudes of the eastern United States, moving from a Maine farmhouse "haunted and haunting" to the cemeteries of New Orleans, a city "perpetually one storm away." And Lena circumscribes each place, lingering in our sightline no matter where we travel.

Lena's first young love is also a queer love, one rejected by Lena's parents and greeted with fraught complication by Lena herself. As in many books about early love, the pair must sneak around, as in "Lena's Summer House in Rockport," where, as the pair sleeps:

> From somewhere along Route 127
> Lena's mother approached.
>
> A neighbor had spotted our car.

Meanwhile, as danger approaches, unknown to the pair, love begins again: "Lena all skin // among scattered pillows / a valiant amateur sailor // began the slow descent along my belly . . ." Here, Pruyn foregrounds a specific peril of young queer love that sets it apart from the broader love-story trope: the risk of the lovers' discovery brings with it not just disapproval or separation from each other, but possible violence or excommunication from the family. We find Lena's mother again in the poem "The Mother," "gazing at me with rage;" we see Lena herself needing an "alibi" just to see the speaker again briefly in "Twenty Minutes at the Clam Shack." No sexual or romantic encounter in *Lena* is truly carefree; the relationship remains closeted throughout the collection:

> Lena, no one knew
>
> not the boys
> not your mother
> not your friends or mine . . .

This forced secrecy further complicates the love-story narrative: while discovery remains dangerous, closeting becomes damning. It pins in the pair, dictating how and when they must show each other love. It keeps them, as their true in-love selves, publicly apart even in mourning, after Lena has died: "Where is her body?" the speaker asks in "Self-Interrogation": "What happened? . . . I wasn't [at the funeral] . . . What, you weren't invited?"

While the pair splits early in the collection, with the speaker leaving Lena "all at once, without warning," their relationship ends permanently with the discovery, then the course of Lena's cancer—a force, introduced nonlinerally by Pruyn alongside the first breakup, that severs the pair a second and final time. We watch as Lena inserts a needle into her belly, "in the same way // she used to attach her cufflinks— / like it was tricky, but habitual," the speaker a close but measurable distance away. In the poem "Flaneur in St. Louis Cemetery No. 1"—once Lena and the speaker have broken up, but before her death—we still track the progression of Lena's illness from afar:

> I found a photo of Lena in a bridesmaid's dress.
> She was anchoring the left

end of an arc of green-clad women—
glasses raised—

and in my present state, of course I zoomed in
to search her chest for the hole,

half-hidden behind the sash.

In death, Pruyn shows us, we must leave Lena all over again. And, as grief's narrative is unpredictable and atemporal, so does the narrative arc of *Lena* deftly twist and reflect, mirroring the unforgivingly circuitous path we must follow as we mourn. *Lena* ends all the way at the beginning, with the speaker imagining the pair, in another "life," meeting as children. "Lena, get up," the speaker orders—or does she plead? "I'll meet you at daybreak // in a grove of grandfather pines . . ."

By keeping the reader's focus "zoomed in" on Lena, Pruyn powerfully evolves the tradition of eponymy: she shows us an entire, yet specific world inhabited by just two people, granting the possibility for broader commentary on love and desire by rendering the singular particularities of a beloved with exacting clarity and resonance. *Lena* reveals a speaker who views her first love through a shifting, unstable kaleidoscope of coming-of-age and loss, who finds more longing instead of simple peace in the wake of the beloved's departure. "[T]he distance between us," she tells us in the poem "In the Vineyard," "the one we'll cross, reestablish, / cross, // reestablish, // too many times to count— / exists even now," even as Lena has gone for good. And the loss remains forever with the speaker, as with Lena's now-absent body, as something still to touch, and to revere: "I still hold it in my hands."

"Who has she made me?" Like the best love stories, *Lena* raises this question not just for the speaker, but for the reader as well. These masterful poems show us that, if love causes our greatest suffering, it also fosters our greatest happiness: and, perhaps most importantly, it creates the place we might also discover ourselves. In *Lena*, Pruyn shows us how to "collapse the map:" how to find, then walk, the path back home.

Acknowledgments

My deepest gratitude to Rachel Mennies and the staff of TTU Press for believing in this collection. I also want to thank my Bennington teachers and mentors for helping me tease out the very first poems of this manuscript, for your words of wisdom and your fine example, and for training my ears. Thank you to my early poetry teachers, Michael Ives and especially Mark Melnicove, for your inspiration, continued friendship, and endless support. Thank you to the Peauxdunque Writers Alliance, my New Orleans krewe, for inviting me in and believing in my poems, and to my New Orleans workshop readers for your invaluable feedback. Thank you to all the readers I have sent these poems to over the past few years. Love, admiration, and gratitude to my Bennington classmates, whose friendship I value beyond measure. Emily Mohn-Slate and Jennifer Stewart Miller, my true friends and poetry soulmates, thank you for your amazing eyes, hearts, minds, and sunrooms, and for making *Lena* the best it could be. Love and gratitude to my giant, big-hearted family, for supporting me and believing in me no matter what, and to Lauren, my best friend and future wife, for everything.

Grateful acknowledgment is made to the editors of the publications in which the following poems, some in alternate versions, first appeared:

AGNI Online: "Maine Morning, Age 5," "Lost Love Lounge"

Salt Hill Journal: "Want"

The Los Angeles Review: "Flaneur in St. Louis Cemetery No. 1"

The Common: "Closeted in Dutchess County," "Twenty Minutes at the Clam Shack"

Poet Lore: "Androgyny"

The Adroit Journal: "Lena's Summer House in Rockport"

CutBank All Accounts and Mixture: A Celebration of LGBTQ Writers and Artists: "Talk," "The Last Time I Saw Her," "A Week Before Christmas"

Liminal Stories, "Aubade"

Border Crossing: "Traveler's Monologue"

Big Big Wednesday: "What Cold Can Do," "The Properties of Where," "Lena, No One Knew"

Bridge Eight: "Elegy for Lena," "Fear and the Ensuing Weather," "Patience"

Coda Quarterly: "Desire Antics," "Eight Truths and a Lie," "The Myth of Cancer," "New Orleans," "Dive"

TINGE Magazine: "The Mother"

Lunch Ticket: "The House on Tator Hill"

Blue Lyra Review: "Flaneur on Royal Street, New Orleans"

Pittsburgh Poetry Review: "Gone"

I.

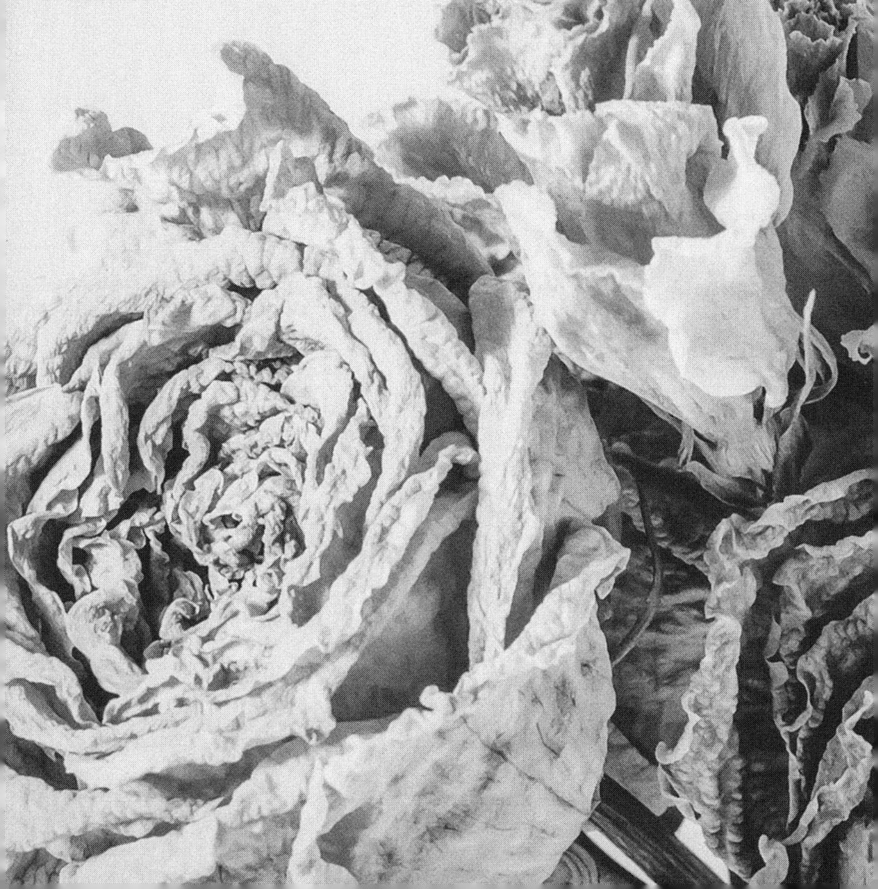

Lena's Summer House in Rockport

On a thin protrusion of Massachusetts rock
surrounded on three sides by sea

down a U-shaped street abutting the beach

in a shingled house   among shingled houses
locked up for winter

chilly and silent except for the hum
of empty refrigerators

in a room at the end of the hall—Lena's room—
we slept. By morning

we had set ourselves adrift

on a white raft   on a gray sea
the cold of which

was a fact that couldn't touch us.

Our little raft

kept twirling and reversing   fore
and aft

above us a swaying

forest of masts
smooth as polished bone.

From somewhere along Route 127
Lena's mother approached.

A neighbor had spotted our car.

Meanwhile   off the port bow   a buoy konged
and Lena   all skin

among scattered pillows
a valiant   amateur sailor

began the slow descent along my belly
into the sheets' folds

where   nervous at first
she would soon taste the salt of the sea lapping

against the damp-dark hull of the boat.

Polaroid

We look up when our names are called:
the camera clicks.

                          We're standing
behind a kindling-stacked
fire pit in the community garden—
too casual,
             the both of us—
my hip cocked, her body leaning
against the handle of a rake.

In the foreground, balanced on a rock,
glinting in the sunset,

a matchbox.

Desire Antics

That first semester we refused to kiss.
Our first, most tumultuous, distance.

For four months we rubbed against
each other's clothed bodies in the dark,

we pressed our foreheads together
and rocked,

we talked nonsense,
chucked ice cubes,
sprayed hoses,
hurled insults,

drove like maniacs, got drunk
and apologized with sodas,

wrestled each other to the grass,
someone pinning, someone's fingers shivering

against the grip.
We even brushed lips

but if we kept them still it didn't count.

She

Strong-jawed blue-eyed blonde

Athletic

Round-hipped

She laughs all the time
                              like an actor   too velvety
She flicks the wisps
of hair from her face with a dainty hand
at least three times a minute
                              Can't sit still
can't keep track of her papers   She drinks
profusely   with good humor
except for when she drinks gin

Want

as in I want to eat her

Eat as in bite her I mean
touch insides

I mean be inside of her

When I reach for her hand
and her eyes get wide
and then I'm alone with the slamming
door

When she says she's sorry
with red birch beer

When she falls asleep on my shoulder

When she glides up slow and says
Get in the car

When   after a swim in the falls   I stumble up
a slick rock dripping wet and hug her

When she buys me a necklace at the county fair

When she knocks again at my door

When she pulls her rain-soaked
shirt off in front of me
then excuses herself to go
call her boyfriend

When she straddles me   dipping her face
closer   closer

When I draw   gently
a gummy bear across her lips
and still she says *no thank* you   I think

I might kiss her   might punch her

The Mother

I met Lena's mother once,
in Lena's kitchen in Concord.

Just shy of five feet, leaning forward with her elbows on the
    counter,
Lena's mother listened as her sons bantered

with the guests, and her husband doled out bottles of water
(quick and jovial, full of facts),

interjecting just once, with what
I can't remember, in a voice that silenced the room.

She hardly seemed to notice me.
It was only later, once she'd found the letter

in Lena's jeans, that I became the enemy.

I've seen her from a distance twice,
both times after an illicit rendezvous, another near-miss.

I've studied family photos in their frames,
holding them close, finding her face.

In dreams I am running from her, hiding
in strange houses, and yet

even when I'm standing close enough to touch her,
her eyes will not land on me,

and so I have no reason to hide.

In the picture they posted of Lena
the night before her first surgery,

she is lying in a hospital bed in a white gown next to her mother,
facing her, kissing her shoulder,

and Lena's mother
(a woman with a mermaid's name)

lies flat on her back with her hand in Lena's,
gazing at me with rage.

The House on Tator Hill

All night the wind strummed the shingles,
while I slept with my jaw like a fist.
She wanted sex first thing in the morning
to the rhythm of the percolator's clicks.

Her aunt had a real Chagall hanging over the piano.
She stocked the freezer with Grey Goose, then traveled for
     months.
We claimed the guest room, the basement, the patio.
We warmed the Veuve on our tongues.

I watched it snow through the window in the spare room
that winter—little no body's window, hardly-used, hardly-seen—
and felt the ecstatic twinge of a poem.
Then April lent March a mouthful of green:

two chocolate meringues and those daffodils, double-busted;
all the times I tripped across the overlapping rugs.
She melted butter in pans while the garden trellis rusted.
Every now and again, my knees bled in the tub.

The pond smelled sour even after we smoked pot
and a doe pranced down and sipped from its edge.
I didn't belong in that house, or in any of its portraits,
but we tried to make a home of its four-poster bed.

Aubade

The first time we slept together
I mean *slept*   we swayed
all night like moored skiffs
shushing water up each other's
smooth fiberglass sides

She'd turn when I'd turn
as if the same wave tipped us
toward the same shore

Far below   a baby whale
spilled free of its mother
in a swirl of red

but the two remained tethered   suspended
even once the cord snapped

Soon enough   light seeped
beneath the rim of the overturned sky

Soon enough   the riffling sea
sharpened to a field of blades

Eight Truths and a Lie

Although I've struggled to find ways to say it,
I never felt shame

for the doughy scent of our breath between sheets

for pinning a raunchy note beneath her windshield wiper

for writing, freshman year, poem after poem about her

for not washing my hands after sex.

Along the same logic,
I never felt guilt, either,

for feeding her cocker spaniel table scraps

for smoking a cigarette while she was in class

for googling her mother because I couldn't meet her

for silencing my ringer

or when I left her, all at once, without warning,
and felt nothing but relief.

Flaneur on Royal Street, New Orleans

A hot Sunday in August.
Men sprinkle the ditches
with buckets full of sawdust,

shoving their brooms grittily
through the narrow, balconied streets.
The potted vines hang swaying in sleep.

The shutters, door-length, stay shut.
I want to leave to go visit her, but I don't.
Occasionally when I call, she picks up.

It's always been about distance
with the two of us.
Why am I now the one to resist?

This street cuts a narrow trench of houses,
speckled with sparrows, bunching,
dispersing. I could get on a bus,

or a plane, or a train,
show up unannounced, and ask
to come in—

What would I say?
I'm sorry, or
It was you who taught me how to stay away.

By the Hudson, years ago, I collected pamphlets
on the town's history, the "Tivoli riots,"
squatting among the one-room library's stacks,

or made sketches of sumac and sycamore,
beauty berry, box bush—I can't remember—
every now and then looking around for her

and pretending I wasn't.
It was over by then. We were barely friends.
But in those days, she was the Hudson.

Back then, if I saw her walking
past my porch on Saturday mornings
in her green jacket, I'd call out, *Good morning!*

willing her to stop in.
Today I gaze up at the power lines,
pondering communication again.

This city's only business is the constant reminding
of the murky Mississippi's winding,
and the river's revenge, and the river's conspiring—

Enough about rivers! Remember the night she called
just before they took her liver out, when I cried
Let me come! But it wasn't the time,

and they hooked her by the ribs like a stripped fish,
and excised the swollen, black-blotted flesh—
meanwhile I rallied friends, east to west,

and begged them to pray, or whatever else,
and instead obsessed over sending daffodils
the transplant ward wouldn't accept.

Now the sky darkens to a mottled mess.
From across the river, rain swarms in sheets.
I run to the car before it keels over—

she doesn't want me there, I tell myself,

slapping past rocketing gutter-spouts,

and it's true, she probably doesn't—

but if I were to touch her again,

could we collapse the map?

Would she taste the warm rain on my skin?

Dive

Lena, your body then
would uncurl like a pinkish fist,
or a bashful-headed fern,
or a tight-furled three-mast ship,

or a breath of April air, sweet
and dewy as a petal's socket
(and sweeter yet to breach
and sweeter still to lock it).

Now your body gushes
with chemicals and tonics,
fungi-steeped pH wash,
needle-point hydraulics

into which, part numb, I slip
every doubt I can think to dip,
my guilty ink, my fear for you,
before sweeping out to sea in you.

New Orleans

I choose life, I choose life, and so I'll stay
in a city perpetually one storm away.

In a whorl of revving dampish breath
I catch wind of her impending death.

Flaneur in St. Louis Cemetery No. 1

I touch my hand to the wall of a tomb,
still warm though the sun just dipped.
The sky is a tattered bloom

draining, then gone.
Through the streets, a steamboat's
calliope warbles

and the cemetery whispers its name:
Number-One, Number-One.

The tombs line this stone-slabbed path
the way houses line a street:

granite cells in grid formation
within the grid of this neighborhood,
the *Vieux Carré,*

which is *itself* enclosed within
the river-warped grid of New Orleans.

I walk slowly along a wall vault,
twice my height.
I bat gently at the ferns

taken root between the bricks.
They burst out from the tombs' slits,
and from the crease of Mary's elbow,

spreading into feathery fields
on the tops of sarcophagi.

Like those sea-floor statues in Cancun,
planted for tourists,
this place erupts in lichen, too,

each tuft a sack
of fungus clutching an alga.

I take comfort in this over-growth.
In right things interlocking.

If Lena had been born two decades later,
perhaps her cells could have latched
onto those nano devices they're just now developing,

loosening to let the drugs through.
Instead all manner of poisons sputter
through her collarbone's plastic mouth.

I've imagined her
clipping her I.V. bags to that wheeled
hatrack in her living room,

leaning back while the concoctions
rush in, as I swim
in the Gulf, or shower off the salt,

my cells' tight
hinges keeping the water out.

Against the west wall,
Jesus hangs from a cross like a slack fish.

To his right, parapet tombs and box tombs,
gabled, stooped,
marked with names rubbed out by rain.

That day,
a few years back, in Upstate,
as we hiked the paths of Ferncliff Forest,

Lena taught me the name
of the strange-fingered sassafras tree,

its leaves three distinct shapes,
and farther on we discovered

an old stone-lined pit built into the hill
like a giant pizza oven.

I crouched inside of it.
The pamphlet didn't explain,
but instead recounted the story

of when Astor, the illustrious previous owner,
went down with the Titanic,
only to be sifted from the Atlantic

a week later,
still hanging from his watch chain.

Why did I come to St. Louis No. 1?

I'm sure it has to do
with studying the laws of positioning.
With the body's

continuous business—
hers, mine.

The perils of proximity.

The calliope plays "You are my Sunshine" now.

I can smell jasmine planted in courtyards

between here and the river;

above me, the blank *whoosh*

of the elevated highway sounds—

sounds again.

I think it was yesterday

I found a photo of Lena in a bridesmaid's dress.

She was anchoring the left

end of an arc of green-clad women—

glasses raised—

and in my present state, of course I zoomed in

to search her chest for the hole,

half-hidden behind the sash.

The Myth of Cancer

I didn't even fully believe it when,
on the last morning of her visit,

she stuck herself in the belly with a needle
filled with blood-thinner, in the same way

she used to attach her cufflinks—
like it was tricky, but habitual.

Even then I still couldn't *feel* her cancer.
Her body was no longer the body I knew,

not because of the scars crisscrossing her midsection,
but because, on that day, years ago,

I had slashed between us an uncrossable gulf.
And the body that had been

mine/not-mine, the breathing-beloved,
the body I clutched

over and over at the peak of pleasure,

I had set at a great distance forever.

II

Traveler's Monologue

I am a Maine farmhouse. A hunkering cape.

I am the farmhouse, haunted and haunting.

I am the armchair in the wood-stove room of the farmhouse, in
    whose crook

I once discovered *the most complete* of all moments,

tilting my head against the wing-backs.

I am the wall of snow, door-shaped in the doorframe.

I am the air that pocked the drift, then kept on blowing.

I am the grave of the livestock veterinarian who once lived in the
    farmhouse.

I am he, calling

his patients from the paddock.

I am the stone wall that partitioned the paddock.

I'm a sick sheep.

A horse with a gash in its mouth.

Patience

One night, freshman year, a few of us
built a bonfire in the community garden.

Lena and I sat apart from the group.
The others were giggling, practicing

prying off beer caps with the butts of lighters,
when she pulled a wooden top from her pocket,

meant for me,
and spun it

into a tawny blur half-lit by the fire.
I must have tried to touch it then,

because Lena blocked my reach
with her forearm, whispering,

Shhh let it finish let it finish.

Elegy for Lena

On Scotland's Orkney Island they recently unearthed
the dirt-caked bones of a fallen dragon:

a 5,000-year-old complex of pathways and buildings,
            another monument among the dozens

already discovered on the archipelago,

like the Ring of Brodgar to the east,
            or the Stones of Stenness,

or that massive, grass-covered tomb, called Maes Howe, to the west,

whose entrance yawns, waiting,
            all year long

to catch the rays of the solstice sun.

*

The crabapple's fat branch
that hung low for years,

blocking the sidewalk on Iberville,
was recently lopped off—

but this morning, distracted,
I flinched and ducked

as if the air would knock me back.

.

Raindrops collect, dive off the lips

of the live oaks' leathery leaves.
Cicadas crescendo, electric,

then fall.
In Burma they continue the search,

crisscrossing the river in rowboats, dragging sticks,
for the world's largest bell, all 60 tons of it,

submerged in the flow.

It's mentioned only twice
in the ancient texts, but the locals know

it's down there somewhere,
upright,

narrowing where the river's arms

ceaselessly stroke it,

its clapper trapped

in a bell-shaped pocket of air.

Lost Love Lounge

Of all the half-lit compartments
on Dauphine Street, I choose
a bar whose name reverses
with each fresh coat of booze,

brick-walled and dank, where hipsters press
quarters into slots,
selecting lights or longs or reds
from the cigarette juke box,

and a boy in a too-loose suit
sings karaoke—
something about a girl's goods
suspended from a peach tree,

how he aches to shake her down,
repeating again and again.
I ask at first for juice and rum;
correct it back to gin.

Then I see her.

      Blond. Pearl-studded.

The room flickers like a grass field—

(her arms out, face tilted)—

beneath a freak wind, reeling

with questions: *Why did she come here?*

How did she—And who's that?

As she comes closer I see

it isn't her—and that's Zach

behind her who moves to greet me—

I hug him like a lost brother.

They reenter the teeming sea,

stumbling into each other.

Back on Dauphine, gin drink

in hand. Diana Ross fades

in the cottony dark.

Swaying past gas-lit arcades,

I recall a night in June

when, by the dashboard light, she asked,

Remember Bunny's daffodils,

that every spring collapsed

beneath their double-blooms?
I ignored the metaphor.
Meanwhile the bald-faced moon
whispered, *Go for the door!*

but she leaned closer, undeterred;
maples ruffled above our heads;
nearby the Hudson clambered
along its glacier-fingered bed.

The street quiets. I turn right,
sniffing the wind for rain.
As I pass, a pit bull riots,
straining against her chain.

The Last Time I Saw Her

Her hand, a cold wing, palm-to-palm
with mine,
and her question I couldn't—

Our love spun in
that first day

        planetary

as if it had swung through a million times
already:

we were what was new.

Mellifluous breeze. Curtains astir.
Both of us holding our breath.

Thank you, I finally said
before continuing,

but it rang like *Fuck you.*

Dead Birds

The first one's feathers, silky threads
teased to fraying,

quivered in the breeze.

A black-throated green warbler,
flying south for the winter—

round body, wings like a humpback's

striated belly,
golden head with streaks of olive,

closed eye muffled

in fluff, beak snapped tight.
Its feet, like wires tipped

with tiny needles, splayed

across the cracks of a brick
softened at the edges with green mildew.

A window victim.

I scooped him up, laid him on a fallen
sycamore leaf,

my cupped hands: the final word.

The second one
I'd heard peeping for weeks

with its siblings, in their nest tucked up

in the rotten siding
from the other side of the wall.

I'd woken each morning

to a bowlful of infant wrens,
their hunger, little beaks

ninety-degrees wide (I imagined)

just to the left of my head.
But this morning, below the nest,

one lay sprawled on the cement.

Irregular juttings;
translucent skin stretched over

a purplish, cold-blooded underworld;

beak as yellow
as a kindergartner's sun;

follicle ridges like bad hair plugs.

Its legs, bent
at ludicrous angles:

a sentence I still can't work out.

Talk

In the blue light of late afternoon,
we take turns trying

to consume,
be consumed.

We've lost by now the power
of language, our phrases a series of

clichéd stutterings—
forever—I love you—mine—

mine—like ramming
against opposite sides of the same wall.

But this afternoon, I say what I mean,

inching my mouth along her soap-
scented skin,

down to that delicate,
earthy place, the threshold of which

I tongue
again and again.

Elegy for a Room

For years, we occupied a room
of our own construction:

Lena with a fistful of snapdragons,
Woodstock in a thunderstorm,

dancing naked in the living room—
we built it as we lived it,

laying floorboards, erecting walls,
plank by plank, knotty

and burled—
my "country dress" more see-through

with every washing,
sex in Florida with a gecko watching,

camping in Maine, a loud mouse
in the pitch-dark—

the only furnishings
a motley of beds, never

officially ours,

between walls we painted

daffodil-yellow, wine-red, blizzard-
white.

Then, she died.

In a roar of silence,
the room's northern wall blew off.
Half the ceiling and the floor ripped off.

Outside, a hot
tangle of foliage,
a measureless drop.

Androgyny

A woman's fingers trembled down my body.
Post punchline she flashed a boyish grin.

She swaggered across the quad like a young man,
wore a plunging neckline to the prom,

swung her muscular
thigh across my hips,

and my hands cupped, without a doubt,
a woman's ass.

A suntanned long-haired boy,
she paddled a canoe all over Canada.

In Rockport one night,
as Van Morrison crooned through the speakers,

her slender hand on my back,
Lena dipped me toward the floor

though she was smaller than I.
A woman's tongue, a boy's lust—

the red dot on her forehead
that every now and then gushed blood.

I never saw it happen,
just as I'll never know for sure she's dead,

though I once touched the foot-long
slashes that stretched

from the top of her sternum to its base
then forked

to encircle her waist, the trail
hot-white and bumpy, as if packed with pebbles

like the trail in "Hansel and Gretel"—
and I traced it to find my way.

Self-Interrogation

What happened?

        If I knew I'd tell you.

        Lena died.

           What happened?

Cancer. You know this.

              Am I the cancer or the anti-cancer?

        Neither. Don't be self-centered.

          When did it begin?

Just after the last time you kissed her.

          Cancer: bad birth. Black—

                  —bloom.

Where is her body?

           If I knew I'd tell you.

          In the ground somewhere. In a coffin.

Did they put blush on her cheeks? Was it open-casket?

        I wasn't there.

                What, you weren't invited?

Just kidding! Just a joke!

        Have you tried googling it?

             Where is her body?

   "Cemeteries near Concord."

        If I knew I'd tell you.

            How do you spell her middle name again?

Call her mother and ask.

       Haha!

That time you called—

           —had to hang—

                —up.

Where is her body?

"Cemeteries near Concord."

You would find it—

    —if you really cared. (Black—

            —bloom.)

Somewhere, a box—

    Where is her body?

    Rotting away between—

          If I knew I'd—

    —panels of satin.

    Where is her—

          Ninety pounds—

Skin like—

    What dress was she—

          —cream

   •

Reader, this was the dream:

In a kitchen filled with people, a tiger and a big dog circle each other, growling. A voice asks, *How will you prevent the fight?* I scream and clap and pull the fire alarm. And when that doesn't work, I swing my leg over the tiger's back like a horse and run him into the yard.

•

Where is her body?

Pinning you beneath the Norway spruces—

Where is her body?

Stirring onions in pans til they turn
translucent—

Where is her body?

Staking tomatoes beside you in the garden, bare feet
in the cool dirt—

Where is her body?

In a green jacket, strolling past
your front porch—

Where is her body?

Diving away to grab the phone—

Where is her body?

       Walking toward you on the brick path,
       folded up in a trench coat—

Where is her body?

       Squirting you with a water gun
       through the open window—

Where is her body?

       Flicking a yo-yo—
       Commanding a sailboat—

Where is her body?

       Napping in your arms, little
       blonde machine, whirring
       and twitching—

III.

Closeted in Dutchess County

Back then she drove a car
red as a dragon.

We bombed along the back roads to Rhinebeck,
my fingers at her crotch.

She took me out to see the birch-skirted
lake Joni Mitchell sings about.

We'd gallivant around Woodstock
sipping hard cider from the farmer's market,

sit kissing on the overlook at sunset,
cruise the Taconic with the windows wide.

Once, at the edge of a field near campus,
I glimpsed a flash of white.

I made Lena pull over, dashed across
to where the vine-tangled forest began.

Lodged in the trunk of a larch, hunched
in the hollow, luminous

beneath leaf muck and rain stains,

a statue of a woman.

In the distance, a car horn called;

the wind whispered *shuhh-shuhh*

through the branch-stitched dome.

A pine needle floated down and caught

in a fold of her robes.

If she was a saint, I didn't know her.

Maine Morning, Age 5

Through my bedroom window,
I spot a peach-colored fish
stuck between stones in the old stone wall.
I imagine she's been beached,

but once I slap through the screened door,
leaping past the snakes' rustle,
I find it's just another rock torn
by a farmer's plunging knuckles

from the landscape's lap,
and propped atop the assemblage.
No longer a *she,* it's a dead fact.
But why is it pinkish-orange?

Bleached by years of sun, I think,
and further bleached by ice.
Grooved with fins of rain, I think.
Mistaken nearly twice.

Lena, No One Knew

not the boys,

not your mother,

not your friends or mine,

how we groped each other one afternoon beneath a row of spruces,

parked between an old sugar maple gutted by lightning

and a rotting barn where two hundred soldiers

once ate, drank, slept and ran repetitive endless drills

to prepare for no one,

near Blithewood,

above the river

that sucked our bodies seaward,

                          no one knew

what we did to each other that day in the shade

and now neither do you

No One Except

the security guard who tapped
on the window with his pudgy knuckle   blushing who

we'd seen approaching with time enough for you
to put your shirt on get behind the wheel
throw your jacket over me and us laughing

for years afterward because as long as it wasn't
your mother's knuckle rapping we were good

Fear and the Ensuing Weather

When she told me about the dream she'd had
about looking down on her own funeral
I didn't ask if she'd seen me there

I figured if the terrifying
thing were to be considered
(my gut rocked by a fist of ice
when she said it) it would be a given

I would be there grieving
wildly
properly

For the rest of the afternoon
like the wave chop at 15 knots
we roiled on the couch

Maybe she felt bad for scaring me
or maybe we'd both caught a whiff
of Time in heat and needed to get each other off

We didn't rush it though
in that room soaked with breath

Well past dusk we rode each other's
bodies like skiffs in the wind

In the Vineyard

Nine years ago, was it, when we
drove three hours to her grandparents'

locked up summer house with no key.

Though we were four months in
to our crazed courtship,

she was still too terrified to kiss me,

and I was too stubborn
to make the first move.

So, for something to do,

we hopped into the bomber, sped
north on 87, cop cars

stationed on the shoulder,

the center console throbbing with the energy it took
for me to not touch her,

some country star on the radio singing

about a girl in cut-offs in the passenger's seat—
her bare feet

on the dash—

and what he aimed
to do with her when they parked.

We turned up the drive to her grandparents' house.

Shades drawn.
Scraggly vineyard rows

sloping down to the trees.

The year's first
snow softening the hill scruff.

In the picture I took,

blurry, black and white,
she slants against the wind in her peacoat

walking the rows,

beneath a gray sky swollen
with our stalling.

And the distance between us—

the one we'll cross, reestablish,

cross,

reestablish,

too many times to count—
exists even now.

I still hold it in my hands.

Twenty Minutes at the Clam Shack

Beneath a chalk-white winter sky,

her diamond studs gleam.

We sit parked in the Clam Shack lot, halfway

between her house and mine,

in her mother's luxury SUV. Her alibi this time:

Christmas shopping for her mother on Newbury Street.

She wears a black, full-length wool coat

unbuttoned at the throat.

I slip my hand under her blouse, which quivers

with heartbeats, trace

the silken blade of her collarbone,

lean down to sniff her neck.

Gulls screeching, flapping, battling

for scraps across the Clam Shack's pavement.

Traffic rushing beyond the chainlink.

As the dashboard clock clicks and dry heat

sighs from the vents, Lena

pushes a button and her seat reclines—she pulls

me toward her, whispering

Come here like she'd snatched up

a pocketknife and sliced

a sliver in the day just for me.

Red Cap

Lena leans against the warm bricks
of the laundromat

red cap tugged low

Her scent   like salt
on the May day's flavors   unlocks—

The young trees
along the sidewalk   the ones

that smell like cum
when they bloom

trembled above us then

Of course we'll see each other
this summer Cass

Her liver   in secret
a fattening gnarl

What Cold Can Do

She's still out there somewhere—
she must be—a child,

asleep belly-down on the rug beside the Christmas tree,

the fireplace a mouth of light
laughing out shadows,

only a hundred or so miles from me

where I lie too, in my old living room in Maine,
my eyes turned toward the fire.

Lena, get up.

Put your coat on.
Get your mittens.

Go out the side door and follow along

the stone wall that arcs across the field,
and keep going.

I'll meet you at daybreak

in a grove of grandfather pines—
thick with snow, shellacked with ice—

and we'll kneel and punch our knuckles, numb

as frozen ponds, down to where
the snow is almost warm

it's so deep and weightless.

Shivering, tipping
mittenfuls between each other's teeth,

we'll eat our fill.

Gone

She let go of my hand

slipped away from the group of us

laughing on the sandy shoulder

Strode on between the black locusts arching over River Road

       fiery-green   heavy with pods

along the stone wall bordering the orchard

she and the boys claimed to have plundered

because it was August   and they were barely nineteen

gripping the apples as they ran

She called back to us   announced

she was going to visit the cemetery

a branch of her family occupied down River Road

just beyond Ferncliff Forest and the fork

those two snaking roads make

      as they touch   diverge   she was gone

The Properties of Where

Somewhere inside the earth

we lie together in darkness

Your coffin   as I knew it would be   is of the finest wood

Forget the quantum

photon/proton/whatever it is

Take instead a conference room

whose occupants halfway through the meeting

begin breathing in unison

a single beast

It's huge down here Lena

well-peopled   root-thick

                                     In the dream

I waited for you on a bridge

and when the battleship made its fancy

turn for the crowd   we both watched

Lena

can you feel the sun in New Orleans today

the sidewalk snipped into a paper

snowflake of shadows

the hard reptilian leaves

Resurrection

1.

Here she is, swiping
a fat brush dipped in Robin's Egg Blue
across plaster, in an apartment
high up in an old brick building
along a small-town Main Street
at the base of which a river sparkles,
white clouds slow-motion
zigzagging across the skylight
all afternoon as she strokes and rolls.

Her girlfriend, the one who stuck by her,
whom I've never met, feeds
butter-yellow fabric beneath the sewing machine's
silver chicken foot.
They are bickering, laughing,
yelling down through the open window
to friends out to drinks on a nearby patio,
and when the light starts fading they trot down
to meet them, holding hands,
glancing for cars before crossing
the street.

2.

Here she is, gripping sheets.
Hauling them up in a whipping
wind, her small
Sperry'd feet braced
against the deck, her face tensed
with ferocity, the sails' metal rings
clanging against the mast.

She shouts now to her brother—
run that jib out!—
and they're off, they're racing
against a dense blue sky—
boat slicing, wind
thrilling, her brother
doing her bidding—as she hops up, winches a line,
loops, tightens, ducks, eases the polished
stick to the left,
her mind a flurried
map of angles as she
scans and adjusts, scans and
adjusts.

3.

Here she is, smashing garlic.
Peeling, chopping, mincing.
She swipes the knife clean with her finger,
she rinses.
She tosses hunks of meat into a pan,
pierces, flips, adds spices.
Her friends mill about in the other room
while her girlfriend plays hostess,
talking and laughing over
soft-playing music.

Across the kitchen, a bowl waits.
It waits for Lena to brace it
with a strong, slender arm,
her other hand clasped
around the mixer's black handle,
her whole body buzzing,
until the egg whites begin lifting their foamy necks
toward Lena's face. Her face:
pinkening, patient.

A Week Before Christmas

approaching dusk,

Lena and I in her dorm room,
draped over the bed, fully dressed,

our hands groping for openings.

She's supposed to be waiting outside for her brother.
They're going to a family party down River Road.

Through the picture window, the dorm's shadow
stretches like a castle across the snow.
Lena's sapphire studs glitter.
Her neck smells like Europe.

                                      I know exactly where to go,
how to make a tent of her still-buttoned
jeans with the back of my wrist—

Her brother's fists

pound against the locked common room door.
Lena leaps up

like reverse lightning, smooths her hair,
kisses me fast and runs out to him laughing.

I don't mind it yet, the door slamming,
the room watching to see what I'll do.

                              Back then I knew
how to hold on,

how to let the cord between us spool out:

Lena's body racing
through the fresh-spread dark.

Praise for Lena

Like a novel, *Lena* unfolds its love poems as a story through time and space. This remarkable first book is emotionally powerful, delicate and earthy at the same time; startling throughout (because of the technical skill of the poet); and yet also deeply familiar, resonant, as it captures the twin experiences of coming-of-age sexuality and profound loss.

• April Bernard

The poems in Cassie Pruyn's *Lena* possess a magnetism owed to an unconstrained heart and intelligence willing to celebrate the pitch fervor of erotic love and to name the unspeakable agony of unjustly losing an estranged beloved to cancer. In lines stylized yet naturally pitched, her poems espouse the kind of dignity gained from loving by way of sacred remembrance; such is the work of any elegy, but here the prestige of language elevates personal anguish to public healing. We relish in the truth-exacting ear of her imagination and the startling intimacy of her mind.

• Major Jackson

Love, obsession, devotion, desire, grief—these are the rivers that run through this remarkable debut collection by Cassie Pruyn who uses that most ancient and stately vehicle—the personal lyric—to narrate not just what it is to meet the beloved and to lose her, but what it feels like to experience love, only to see the beloved dissipate and die. The love between these two women is chronicled here with devotion, intelligence, tenderness, and a spike of rage. This is a moving, muscular, finely wrought collection and a memorable chronicle of the mind and spirit making beauty and music from the senselessness of loss.

• Mark Wunderlich